Mindful Thirukkural

Kathiravan Krishnamurthi

Published By

BOOK DETAILS

Title	Mindful Thirukkural
Author's Name	Kathiravan Krishnamurthi
	Mail ID:
	kathiravan.krishnamurthi@gmail.com
Book Size	5.5 X 8.5
Pages	116
Published by	MIN E KAVI (மின்கவி)
Publisher details	MIN E KAVI (மின்கவி)
	(E-Development & Digital Publishing)
	www.minekavi.com
	Phone: 9626227537
Edition	I
ISBN	978-93-6274-320-6
Copyrights:	© Author

Foreword

I was pleasantly surprised when our friend Kathir (Kathiravan Krishnamurthi) requested me to write a foreword for his book *Mindful Thirukkural.* The underlying theme of the book is familiar to me; it touches on some aspects of psychology and psychotherapy within my professional domain, which I have been working in for years since completing my M.D. in the United Kingdom. Kathir, an engineer, has connected the maxims of Valluvar to mindful practices in a unique way. He examines Valluvar's ideas on the human mind and its cultivation through the practice of aRam.

His thesis here is that Valluvar has laid down a path to mindfulness in *Thirukkural,* which was written 2,000 years ago. A nuanced view is presented on understanding Valluvar's first chapter. Kathir has interpreted the chapter as meditation, although it is often taught as "Praise of God." Meditation is training that aims to focus the mind on an anchoring object. Kathir uses Valluvar's maxims to explain how meditation can relieve us from stress and worries. He connects the first chapter to the body of Valluvar's work well, allowing the reader to gain a better understanding of the book.

The reader can easily identify the interesting aspects of the book. The subject is a little complex but has been simplified with anecdotes and real-life stories. A unique feature of the book is that Kathir has familiarized himself with modern psychological terms and practical techniques, and relates them to *Thirukkural.* For example, the chapter on distress tolerance resonates well with Cognitive Behavior Therapy techniques.

Finally, I recommend the book to all readers interested in *Thirukkural* and mindfulness. Some of the techniques and methods described in the book in connection with Valluvar's vision for personal and societal development agree with modern perspectives. I extend my best wishes for the book's success and for the author's future endeavors.

Dr. Radhika Murugesan, MBBS, MRCPsych, CCT (UK)

Consultant Psychiatrist,

Founder & CEO,

Chennai Minds.

Preface

Valluvar, the ancient Tamil poet who wrote *Thirukkural*, a classic poetic work on the art of living, speaks to our minds both directly and indirectly. In the first chapter of *Thirukkural*, Valluvar presents a divine symbol of infinite virtue, knowledge, and compassion, namely, lotus feet. His starting point is meditating with this symbol. The succeeding chapters take us through the steps of mindfulness practice, which lay out a path that emphasizes the practice of virtue. *Thirukkural* is written in the Tamil language. It is full of metaphors and analogies and is written in a direct but terse style.

I have observed that though readers of *Thirukkural* appreciate the wisdom of the maxims, they often do not notice how they are all connected. However, it is these interconnections that enable the perceptive reader to discern the mind model underlying the verses. In this small book, we will understand the mind model that Valluvar builds in *Thirukkural* and learn how to apply it in our daily life. We will begin by learning how to meditate, how to overcome the obstacles that litter the path of virtue, and how to practice mindful methods that build our tolerance to distress. As we progress through the book, we will discover some of Valluvar's mystical insights into the power of the smile. We will understand the need for compassion and social awareness, and learn how to condition ourselves to achieve the goal of mindfulness: a sublime mind.

Dear reader, we invite you to join us on Valluvar's journey to mindfulness.

Thanks are due to Ms. Subhashini Siva and Dr. R. Prabhakaran for reading the book and offering helpful suggestions. I am grateful to Santhosh Mathew Paul—copyeditor, classmate, and friend—who made valuable contributions to the book by copyediting it and offering additional editorial inputs.

Introduction

Today, we see scientific and technological advances all around us. New gadgets, services, and tools help us in many ways. Yet, these advances do not touch the fundamentals of our life. We all have emotions, responsibilities, and commitments. We seek joy and fulfillment, just like our parents and grandparents. They may ask us to read ancient classics that teach us lasting values and life lessons, but we do not find those books easy to read. Ancient classics are written in a language that is very different from the language we use today. Older people cherish these classics because they value the stories from them that were narrated by teachers and community leaders. Many of them benefited by applying the lessons they learned from these stories. However, older people may not always be around to share their experiences and stories. How can our children and grandchildren benefit from these stories and learn the lessons they teach?

Thirukkural was written in Tamil about two thousand years ago by Valluvar. The work consists of 1,330 concise maxims on the art of living and has gained a lot of attention worldwide. The ideas in *Thirukkural* are just as timeless as the philosophies of Plato, Socrates, and Aristotle, and they can be appreciated and applied even today.

Often, we rely literally on commentaries and translations to learn *Thirukkural*. Commentators have provided many interpretations of Valluvar's work. We find philosophical depth and profundity of thought in his maxims. One of the topics he addresses that is relevant for us today is our mind. Though Valluvar addresses the mind and its wellness, not much work has been done on this aspect of *Thirukkural*. I would like to share some of my learnings on Valluvar's thoughts on the mind, its development, and its wellness. In this book, we will read some of Valluvar's ideas on psychology and therapy. We will also see how these ideas connect to modern views on the mind and its wellness.

Recently, I came across an online article on smile therapy written by a practicing psychologist (Kraft and Pressman 2012). The author describes how smiling can help people deal with distress and refers to the associated research and findings. In the experiment, subjects simulated a smile by biting on a chopstick. The results of the study showed that the heart rates of the subjects decreased faster after performing a stressful task when they smiled than when they did not smile. This story reminded me of a classical maxim in *Thirukkural* that I had read in school: "When in distress, smile gently; what follows cannot be harder." In this book, we will see other examples of how *Thirukkural* bridges ancient wisdom and modern psychological research.

After I discovered the correspondence between smile therapy and a maxim in *Thirukkural,* I searched the work for more examples of how to cultivate the mind. This book presents the findings of my search, slide by slide. Much like an athlete preparing for a long run by warming up, we see the poet using meditation as the first step to cultivating the mind. He then lays out the path for cultivating the mind and describes the obstacles along the path. Once we clear the obstacles from our path, we will see a long road ahead. We can advance on this road with steps such as practicing gratitude, forbearance, compassion, and social responsibility. If all goes well, at the end of this road we will be rewarded with a sublime mind, which is the end goal of mind cultivation according to *Thirukkural.*

Contents

1.

Meditation in Thirukkural

Brilliant things happen in calm minds. Be calm. You're brilliant.

– Anonymous.

A woman had it all: kids, a loving husband, and a happy home. She still felt something was missing. One day, she shouted at her kids for no apparent reason. Realizing that she was unhappy, she consulted both a psychologist and a psychiatrist. They felt that no treatment was necessary, but she remained unhappy. Taking matters into her own hands, she decided to try meditation classes. She liked the classes and began to feel fulfilled and at peace with herself.

She meditated on a special place that was in a jungle beside a waterfall, surrounded by nature and gentle animals; here, she was totally accepted and free. She found that when she went to her special place during meditation she could think clearly.

Externally, nothing had changed for her. As soon as she succeeded in calming her mind, she began to appreciate everything around her. She had turned her life around. She then trained herself and became a meditation teacher so that she could change other people's lives.

Reading this true story (Victoria n.d.), we understand that meditation was the solution to the lady's anxieties. Valluvar too conveys the benefits of meditation in *Thirukkural*. He describes meditation in the first chapter of his book. To help us unravel his message, let us first understand the basics of meditation.

What Is Meditation?

Meditation is a practice of mindfulness, or focusing the mind on a particular object, thought, or activity to train attention and awareness, and achieve a mentally clear and emotionally calm and stable state (Walsh and Shapiro 2006). It is a discipline that involves deep relaxation and focused attention. Meditation is an attempt to clear your mind of its normal rush of cluttered thoughts. We do this by refocusing our attention on a single thought, phrase, object, or activity that is usually called the "focal point" of our meditation. Meditation is found in every major religion and in most cultures, e.g., Taoist and Hindu yogas, Jewish Hassidic and Kabalistic dillug and tzeruf, Islamic Sufism's zikr, Christian contemplations, Buddhist meditations, and Confucian quiet-sitting (Walsh 1999).

When we meditate, we spend time with our mind. We take time out of our busy days to shut out the world, sit in a quiet place, and concentrate on our chosen meditative focal point. Doing this helps us become more aware of our thoughts, act more compassionately toward ourselves and others, and connect with the present moment.

The Role of Symbols in Meditation

Symbols are a clever way of displaying an external sign of an internal meaning. They form an important part of many Indian traditions like Siddha, Yoga, and Tantra. These symbols represent the connections ancient people developed with natural forces through their experiences. In modern prose, symbols are found in literary devices such as the simile and the metaphor; for example, in the simile "My love's like a red, red rose" (a line from a Robert Burns poem), the rose is a symbol of love. Allegories use symbolic meaning in more complex ways. For example, in *Animal Farm* by George Orwell, animals represent different groups of people.

Meditation practitioners use symbols to access inner forces, elevate awareness, develop positive qualities, and find deeper meaning and insight. Hence, practitioners must know some of these commonly used symbols and their spiritual significance.

Let us look at some of these **symbols** and examine how Valluvar used them to *progress in mindfulness practice.*

Lotus Feet as a Symbol

For thousands of years, Eastern philosophers have used the lotus as a symbol of the feet of exalted beings.

They use figurative language, metaphors, and analogies in many of their teachings.

They use the image of lotus feet to represent the teachings of noble mentors and the idea of meditating on lotus feet to connect with these teachings.

Reflecting on the above, I thought about a Tamil hymn by the famous saint Ramalinga Swamigal (1823–1874) that we had learned in school:

ஒருமையுடன் நினது திருமலரடி நினைக்கின்ற
உத்தமர் தம் உறவு வேண்டும்
உள்ளொன்று வைத்துப் புறம்மொன்று பேசுவார்
உறவு கலவாமை வேண்டும்

I want the company of noble people who meditate on
your lotus feet with single-minded devotion;
I want to avoid relationships with deceitful people
who think
something in their hearts but speak the opposite.

Unaware of the mystical significance of "lotus feet," I had
interpreted the hymn in a very literal way as a child.
Now I know that St. Ramalinga wants us to follow the
principles underlying the symbol. He lists all of them in his
work.

Nammazhvar (8th century CE), one of the founding Bhakti
saint-poets of Vaishnavism, refers to meditation (focusing
the mind) on the feet of Maal (Vishnu). In his invocation
hymn in *Thiruvaaymozhi*, he wrote:

உயர்வு அற உயர் நலம் உடையவன் எவன்? அவன்
மயர்வு அற மதி நலம் அருளினன் எவன்? அவன்
அயர்வு அறும் அமரர்கள் அதிபதி எவன்? அவன்
துயர் அறு சுடர் அடி தொழுது எழு என் மனனே

My mind, lift yourself up to the dazzling, *distress-dispelling* feet of the One,

who is the Lord of the ever-alert *Eternal Heroes*,

who is the natural repository of super-excellent traits

which cut out all fatigue, and

who granted *wisdom-love* and rid me of *ignorance*,

leaving no trace of it behind.

> Note on Reverence
>
> *adi* means "foot" in Tamil. It is usually referred to as a pair (*adiyiNai*) or in its plural form *adikaL* (அடிகள்). *adikaL* is used metaphorically to refer to exemplary persons such as saints and exemplars who are followed because they provide valuable guidance. For example, the ancient Tamil

text *Silappathikaram* refers to a female Saint KavunthiyadikaL, who helped the heroine, Kannagi. Tamils affectionately referred to Mahatma Gandhi as Gandhi adikaL.

Now that we understand the significance of terms and symbols, we can move on to learn what *Thirukkural* says about meditation and cultivating mindfulness.

The Feet as the Focal Point

In his first chapter, Valluvar gives readers ideas they can use to prepare themselves for mindfulness through devotion. In his opening maxim, after stating that the

Supreme is pre-eminent, he begins to explain His attributes.

The First Maxim

The poet begins the first chapter with a powerful analogy: Just as the first letter in the alphabet is "a," the Lord is first in the world. The Lord's nature and relationship with the world is conveyed in the first maxim. The Lord is primary and basic. Human beings throughout history and across cultures have given many names for the Supreme Being: Siva, Allah, Kali, Yahweh, Jehovah, etc. Valluvar addresses the Supreme as the first (*aathi*) such one (*pagavan*) in the world. The word *pagavan* comes from the root *pagu* (divide, split, dispense, apportion). Valluvar has used *paga* and *pagavu* to mean "split" and "divide" in a few places. The Lord, Valluvar's Primal Deity or Supreme Being, knows the good and bad deeds of human beings and rewards them accordingly.

அகர முதல எழுத்தெல்லாம் ஆதி
பகவன் முதற்றே உலகு (01)

"A" is the first letter of languages,
the Primal Deity is first through all domains (01)

In the second maxim, Valluvar sees the Supreme Being as the embodiment of pure knowledge. Because the Lord possesses pure knowledge, Valluvar calls him Valarivan. People of the Indian subcontinent and many tribes worldwide imagine the Supreme in human or material form. We can easily think of him as the leader of the universe and imagine him as our own lookalike. Nobody can draw or carve the omnipresent, symbol-less, aspect-less Lord. If the Lord is the embodiment of the intellect, how can we see him in the mind's eye? In this hymn, to help us visualize the Supreme, Valluvar uses the symbol of the feet to represent Him. We can then seek His grace and blessings by worshipping the symbol (feet).

கற்றதனால் ஆய பயனென்கொல் வாலறிவன்
நற்றாள் தொழாஅர் எனின். (2)

What profit have they derived from learning if
they fail to meditate
on the good feet of learned Valarivan? (2)

Valluvar's Supreme Being, Valarivan, is believed to have perfect knowledge that is free of doubts. The poet wonders, what is the use of learning and education if one does not seek the grace and blessings of the One who possesses supreme knowledge?

These verses target all learners, even those who are more knowledgeable than the average person within an organization or country. Valluvar desires that all humans, however learned they may be, seek immortality and fame through humility and modesty. We can spend a lifetime observing how things work and searching for explanations. Yet even a lifetime is insufficient to fathom it all. The Supreme Being as a Valarivan is imagined to be a person who possesses "perfect knowledge" and whose blessings we seek; otherwise, what is the point of our learning?

Usually, meditation is a learned art. We submit ourselves to, listen to, and follow a knowledgeable guide (Guru, Teacher) to learn the fundamentals. We follow people who are led by knowledge. Having prepared ourselves and committed ourselves to following the learned Guru, we need to understand the fundamental mechanism of meditation. We will explore this in the next section.

Transcend the Pleasures of the Senses

We need to cultivate our minds to focus. How do we train our mind?

The first step is to move beyond the pleasures of the five senses. Every sense organ operates independently and perceives only a single dimension of reality. These organs may change their mode of operation or work sequentially, but they never unite and work together. When one sees, one only sees. An attempt to see, hear, touch, and taste at the same time produces only a blurred or foggy image or impression. That is why when you want to concentrate on a piece of music, you close your eyes to channelize all your attention through your ears. Similarly, when you want to focus on one object, you block out your senses and enter your mind. This is *meditation.*

Valluvar wants us to follow the path of the one who has mastered the five senses: touch, hearing, smell, sight, and taste. He calls the Lord Ainthaviththaan, the one who has mastered his senses. *Ainthu* means five, and *Aviththal* here denotes the act of conditioning. Conditioning our senses makes it possible to focus our minds. However, we can only achieve this with practice and mastery, and when we limit distractions around us as when we meditate.

பொறிவாயில் ஐந்தவித்தான் பொய்தீர் ஒழுக்க நெறிநின்றார் நீடுவாழ் வார். (6)

Follow the path of Ainthaviththaan, who sublimated

the five senses and led a disciplined life to

ensure lasting survival (6)

Aviththal has two meanings in Tamil: "to repress, to extinguish" and "to cook." Cooking here means elevating something to a more sublime state by removing the dross and distilling the essence and making it last for a long time. Idli *Avithaan* means to cook the rice cake. Cooking the rice into a cake in an oven extends its longevity. It becomes more palatable and easily digestible (Kuppusamy 2022). In summary, this is the process of transcendence at work. Similarly, when all the five senses are refined (cooked) and their limitations are removed (repressed, extinguished), they work together, like instruments in an orchestra playing in unison (Kuppusamy 2022).

The above maxim (Maxim 6) states that our perception becomes clear when we turn on only one sense, because we can use it with singular focus and clarity. By concentrating on a specific thought and eliminating unwanted distractions, we can extinguish intrusive thoughts. The implication is that to train our mind, we need to shut out distractions and other intrusive thoughts that hinder our progress toward mindfulness. Next, Valluvar suggests meditation as a means of relief from distress.

Maugham and Meditation: An Anecdote

We have read about the sublimation of the five senses and a simple meditation technique centered on it. The famous novelist Somerset Maugham visited India in 1936. He wrote about his experiences in India in an essay titled "The Saint," which was published in an essay collection called *Points of View* (Maugham 1958). The "saint" referred to in the title of the essay is Ramana Maharshi, whom Maugham met in Tiruvannamalai.

In Calcutta, Maugham met a biologist who had married an American woman. The biologist practiced meditation for one or two hours every day. His wife narrated the following anecdote to Maugham. The biologist and his wife had recently traveled to a science conference by night train. Their carriage was crowded and noisy, and the wooden seats were hard and uncomfortable.

When the train started, the biologist entered Samadhi (a term used for greater than 28 minutes of unaltered attention to the centering object or anchor in meditation). The noise in the carriage and the uncomfortable seat did not bother him, as he was in a deep meditative state. The biologist did not emerge from it until the next morning when they reached their destination.

His wife, however, could not sleep that night because the others in the carriage talked and ate throughout the night. She had a headache in the morning, but her husband was fresh and alert. After reaching their hotel, she collapsed on the bed. He, however, worked throughout the day "as though he had slept the night through on his own comfortable bed at home."

Five Senses Grounding

A form of meditation that is practical and calming and helps us appreciate the present moment is called **five senses grounding** (Gelpi 2023). Using this technique, we focus on one sense at a time during meditation. For example, we might go to the woods and meditate by concentrating on the leaves, branches, flowers, trunks, streams, and shrubs.

We then close our eyes and listen to birds chirping and streams gushing. Next, we feel the air and our clothes hugging us, and the cool breeze. We then smell the leaves, flowers, and pine wood. Finally, we close our eyes and taste and relish a mint. This is called grounding the senses; we ground our vision to hear. When we are distressed due to high levels of anxiety, all our energy flares up and exhausts us. Although all our senses are turned on, our perception is clouded. We may perceive higher levels of danger and not enjoy the good things around us. We gasp for breath as we get exhausted. In five senses grounding, we lower our energy level by exercising only one sense at a time. This has a calming effect on us, and we can train ourselves to fully enjoy the moment mindfully.

Meditation Offers Relief from Distress

Anxious persons are fearful, restless, and have trouble concentrating. They experience increased heart rate, sweating, and trembling, and are always worried. Anxiety can lead to the release of stress hormones, which increase heart rate and blood pressure. If this occurs repeatedly, the blood vessels may get inflamed, leading to hardened artery walls, unhealthy cholesterol levels, and other problems. In Maxim 7, Valluvar offers meditation as a viable solution.

தனக்குவமை இல்லாதான் தாள்சேர்ந்தார்க்
கல்லால்
மனக்கவலை மாற்றல் அரிது. (7)

**Distress does not afflict those who meditate
at the feet of the peerless Lord (7)**

As we discussed earlier, one of the ways of calming the mind is to meditate. In Maxim 7, Valluvar urges us to focus on the symbolic feet of the compassionate Lord in order to remove distractions and worries. Here, the feet become the centering object. The incomparable person that Valluvar presents has good qualities such as self-control over all his faculties. Focusing on the feet (அடி, தாள்) helps one follow the ideals of, and the path laid out by, the peerless Lord. We will describe those ideals and path in our chapters.

Overcoming distress through meditation makes us feel better. We are more ready to face turbulence in life. In the following section, Valluvar reinforces the idea of overcoming troubles with a vivid metaphor.

Placement on a Flower?

In the following maxim, we see a consummate poet conveying a lesson using figurative speech:

> மலர்மிசை ஏகினான் மாணடி சேர்ந்தார்
> நிலமிசை நீடுவாழ் வார். (3)

> The Lord, who resides in our mind (flower) and
> whose glorious feet we meditate on,
> we follow to live long (3)

To understand Valluvar's maxims, sometimes we must observe a pattern. Does Valluvar's Primal Deity place Himself on a flower, and do we touch His feet to live longer on Earth? Well, when we studied Maxim 3 in middle school, I had that literal idea. Now, as an adult, with my knowledge of mystic symbolism and meditation, I interpret the maxim as follows.

A cultured and gentle mind is likened to a flower, which stays afloat when there is water in the pond. "A flower rises with the water level," Valluvar says elsewhere in his book (Maxim 595). A lotus flower does not sink when the pond fills. Similarly, noble minds do not sulk when confronted with troubles; they rise to the occasion and face the situation calmly. The Lord can instill Himself in the minds of noble men so that they think about Him, are led by Him, and seek Him out in every way. He is the source of perfect knowledge (Maxim 2). Following Him means clinging to the symbol (feet) we talked about earlier. Valluvar's message is that such a devoted person who is led by knowledge and virtue can transcend the pleasures of the senses (as described earlier) and will know how to face trouble; he or she will not sulk but work out ways to deal with difficulties and lead a long and happy life. But how is this long and happy life achieved? We will find out in the following chapters.

As we saw earlier, the approach to a long and happy life boils down to conditioning our mind through meditation to deal with our worries. Next, Valluvar calls the Primal Deity a righteous and compassionate entity. Following Him will help us navigate the stormy waters in our life on Earth, be resourceful enough to lead a family, earn wealth, and achieve happiness. In the same chapter, he advocates a righteous path with a compassionate outlook.

Righteousness and Compassion

Toward the end of his first chapter, in Maxim 8, Valluvar says that meditation at the feet of an infinitely virtuous and compassionate Lord gives us the strength and will to overcome the challenges and troubles in our life.

அறவாழி அந்தணன் தாள்சேர்ந்தார்க் கல்லால்
பிறவாழி நீந்தல் அரிது. (8)

Difficult to cross the seas of trouble—without
meditating at the
feet of the virtuous and compassionate Lord (8)

Valluvar uses the metaphor of an ocean to convey depth and vastness, and talks about two oceans: first, *the ocean of righteousness*, and second, *the sea of troubles* (challenges in gathering resources, establishing family, love, relationships, etc.). Valluvar says the Primal Deity is an ocean of virtue and calls Him compassionate and kind (*anthaNan*). The message of Maxim 8 is that it is difficult for those who do not follow His virtuous and compassionate ways to navigate the vast trouble-filled world.

Meditating constantly on the infinitely virtuous, compassionate, and kind Supreme Being makes us virtuous, compassionate, and kind. The idea is that we become what we think about. "What you think you become, what you feel you attract, what you imagine you create," said the enlightened Buddha. Some studies have revealed the benefits of compassion and kindness meditation.

To detect rapid changes in brain activity, scientists use electroencephalography (EEG) sensors—those little scalp electrodes that look like a shower cap. These sensors allow scientists to detect rapid electrical fluctuations called brain waves.

Experiments on Tibetan monks engaged in compassion meditation reveal induction of gamma waves, which are correlated with happiness (Ricard et al. 2014).

Meditation and Brain Waves

Brain waves are classified according to the number of times per second that they rise and fall. Different frequencies are associated with different states of consciousness.

Alpha waves are the soft lighting of consciousness. In the alpha state, we feel relaxed and calm, not overly fixated on any specific thought or action, yet awake and alert. Mindfulness meditation has been shown to boost alpha levels in the brain, even when persons are not actively meditating. This could partly explain why we sometimes feel calmer and more relaxed after a meditation session, and why long-term meditators report feeling more at ease overall.[11]

The other scientific finding I love is the link between increased gamma waves and loving-kindness or compassion meditation. Gamma waves are the fastest brain

---

waves, oscillating at a frequency of 25-100 times per second. A study of Tibetan monks highly practiced in loving-kindness meditation found that their gamma waves were off the charts, higher than those of any humans previously recorded.[12] This led to one of the monks, a man named Matthieu Ricard, being dubbed "the happiest man in the world."

The Path to Follow and Practice

We have seen that *Thirukkural* exalts the Primal Deity, who conditions the five senses; who is an ocean of righteousness, kind and compassionate; and who is learned and knowledgeable.

That is, Valluvar's godhead possesses the attributes that he wants us to cultivate. Valluvar refers to the path that must be followed to achieve these attributes as *aRam*. Valluvar covers all the details of *aRam*—the path of virtue—in *Thirukkural*.

He highlights the qualities that help remove the mental clutter that can impede our progress on the path. Valluvar knows that it difficult to eliminate distractions, and to achieve this, he recommends the practice of meditation centered around the virtuous and compassionate Lord.

To meditate on the Lord's feet is to follow His footsteps and travel on His virtuous path.

We practice meditation by imagining a centering object when we are calm, quiet, and rested. We close our eyes and meditate with the centering object in mind.

This centering object could be a simple rock or stone, a small idol, or even a pendant around our neck.

When we are worried or feel stressed, we can shift our focus away from our worries by touching the pendant and taking deep breaths.

During devotional meditation, we contemplate the Lord's virtues, qualities, kindness, greatness, compassion, and wisdom, all of which are described by Valluvar in his maxims.

We can chant a maxim and use even an idol or picture of Valluvar as the centering object.

In the following chapter, we will see how Valluvar addresses the problem of removing the obstacles to the healthy cultivation of the mind.

Summary: Meditate on the righteous and compassionate Lord.

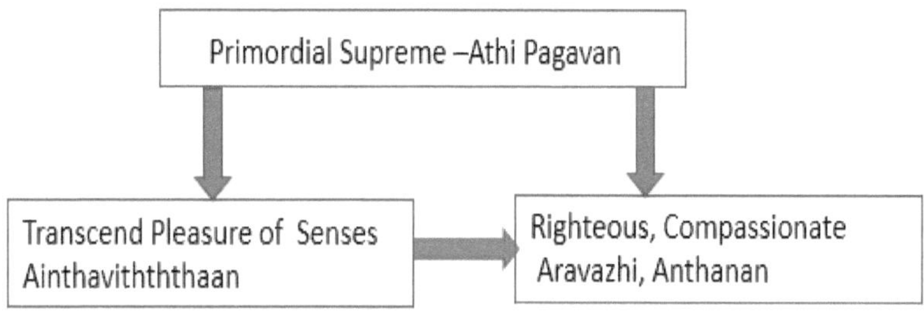

Meditate on the Righteous and Compassionate Lord

2.

The Path and Its Hurdles

If you are on the right path, it will always be up hill

– Henry B. Eyring

aRam is a special word that indicates good deeds. It is formed from two words: *aRu* (அறு) and *am* (அம்). The first word means "cut through." aRam is used to cut away obstacles and clear the **path** ahead. As we travel through life, we face many problems. aRam helps us deal with these hurdles. aRam is a collection of disciplinary methods devised by the wise to help practitioners lead a fulfilling life. Over time, the word *aRam* has expanded to convey powerful connotations such as goodness, charity, and even justice. aRam encompasses the many good qualities needed to lead a successful and happy life. In general, aRam embodies virtues and the good deeds that result from them.

Thoughts are the basis of orderly conduct and discipline. Pure thoughts lead to good and kind words, which in turn lead to good actions (deeds). Thoughts are static; words and actions are the dynamic counterparts of thought. For thoughts to be pure, the mind should be free of blemishes; actions will then follow the righteous path of aRam. Valluvar lays down a philosophical definition of aRam in Maxims 34 and 35:

மனத்துக்கண் மாசிலன் ஆதல் அனைத்தறன்
ஆகுல நீர பிற. (34)

Right action is purity of mind—everything else is fruitless (34)

He says, "The spotless mind is the fountain of righteousness; everything else is just vanity." He further goes on to define the "spotless mind" in Maxim 35:

அழுக்காறு அவாவெகுளி இன்னாச்சொல் நான்கும்
இழுக்கா இயன்றது அறம் (35)

Envy, greed, anger, bitter words—virtue
is devoid of all four (35)

Maxim 35 describes virtue in terms of the absence of the following negative qualities: envy, greed, anger, and the use of bitter words. Whereas Maxim 34 talks about the attributes of an unpolluted mind, Maxim 35 deals with the pollutants, that is, the habits and qualities that cause a person to deviate from the path of aRam. Thus, Maxim 34 defines aRam in terms of its attributes, whereas Maxim 35 lists some flaws that must be negated before one can achieve the ideal: a spotless **mind.** Many commentators have looked at Maxims 34 and 35 as a pair: the first maxim talks about a spotless mind, and the second suggests a possible way to achieve it.

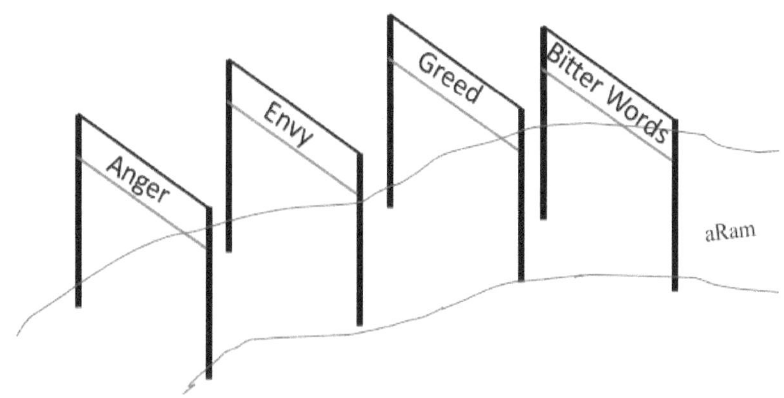

As we proceed to read Valluvar, we find that he implicitly draws a picture of righteousness that would bring long-lasting wealth and fame for the adherent; however, the deviant could experience a downfall. The strong foundation of his aRam is a faultless mind free of greed, jealousy, anger, and hurtful words. aRam is freely adopted as a goal-oriented ethic by a person who believes in its utility; it is followed by one who is liberated, and its practice brings boundless joy. Valluvar's virtues are thus based on the ideals he envisages. An individual who follows these ideals will experience enduring joy in his or her life.

aRam and the Joyous Mind

Thirukkural asserts that the fountain of joy should have flowed down a righteous path, otherwise the joy will be temporary.

People attain joy by various means: a good name and good work can bring joy, wealth and income can bring joy, alcohol can relax people, the ability to wield power and influence can bring joy; sensual pleasure can yield joy, and even gambling can give joy.

Even revengeful people feel a momentary happiness.

However, true joy should be obtained through righteous means. Good deeds and a disciplined life will bring joy. Even wealth earned with the intention of bringing joy should be obtained in a righteous manner.

So, the pursuit of righteousness can bring joy through a variety of legitimate activities that harm nobody.

These activities could span different fields such as entertainment, money management, compassion, service, charity, power, dance, sports, meditation, and so on.

அறத்தான் வருவதே இன்பம் மற்றெல்லாம்
புறத்த புகழும் இல (39)

Right action brings happiness—the rest
earn no fame (39)

Sweet Words Spoken with a Smile

முகத்தான் அமர்ந்துஇனிது நோக்கி
                        அகத்தானாம்
இன்சொல் இனதே அறம் (93)

Sweet words, flowing from the mind, conveyed
with a
smile, have virtue in them (93)

"Virtue is uttering sweet words with love in our heart." Here, *Thirukkural* in the original uses "sweet" (*inithu*) twice, once for sweet countenance and then for sweet words. Here, the sweetness of the look together with love emanating from the mind (*agam*) is described. Eye contact is also noted, conveying the unity of mind and body (via the eye). The poet who called for purity of mind in Maxim 34 again invokes the mindful utterance of kind words. He ends the maxim with aRam, thus making "kind words" emanating from a faultless mind a manifestation of virtue.

Many authors emphasize that charity is part of the practice of aRam. We may also think that we always have to give gifts to practice aRam. For the wealthy, it is easy to give money and gifts. Valluvar brings "smiling and uttering kind words" to the forefront of practicing virtue. He wants us to practice charity not only by giving money or gifts but also by using heartfelt sweet words.

Light of Grace

Graceful people are blessed with a light that enables them to navigate through dark times without difficulty. In a world of grace, there is no room for evil acts like lying, killing, and stealing. The state of bliss is easily attained when all evil actions causing suffering are removed. Graceful people do not engage in violence.

A world without grace would be full of war, strife, and suffering. Since such a world is often referred to as a world of darkness, it can be interpreted as the manifestation of evil.

அருள்சேர்ந்த நெஞ்சினார்க்கு இல்லை இருள்சேர்ந்த
இன்னா உலகம் புகல் (243)

Ignorance and darkness—will never approach the graceful mind (243)

The ignorant and dark world Valluvar refers to here is full of suffering caused by unkind people who do not wish to do good.

Instead, they act in harmful ways without any fear of consequences.

Not Being Jealous

Nature has its characteristics. Water is cool. Fire is hot. Valluvar wants us to develop a nature that is free of jealousy.

This nature, he says, sets us on a disciplined and orderly path for life. Valluvar wants people not to brood jealously over what others acquire and achieve. He wants freedom from jealousy to be made part of a disciplined way of life (161).

ஒழுக்காறாக் கொள்க ஒருவன்தன் நெஞ்சத்து
அழுக்காறு இலாத இயல்பு (161)

Freedom from jealousy is

a path to a disciplined life (161)

Recall that jealousy is one of the blemishes of a spotless mind that Valluvar talks about earlier (in Maxim 35).

Just as we avoid a path filled with stones and thorns and frequented by robbers and wild animals, we similarly avoid the path of jealousy. The path used by the poet, marked by discipline and good conduct (*ozhukkam*), is called ozhukkaaRu.

Removing Anger from Our Mind

Depression can make us feel angry with others. Anger in our mind can damage our relationships, isolating us.

If we are full of bitterness and resentment, the intensity of our efforts will be blunted, making it is difficult for us to get what we want.

Valluvar says:

உள்ளியது எல்லாம் உடன்எய்தும்
உள்ளத்தால்
உள்ளான் வெகுளி எனின் (309)

If anger can be removed from within our minds, we
can achieve all our objectives (309)

If we do not become angry, we can think and act calmly. Becoming a hate-free, calm person simplifies one's goals, which makes wish fulfillment easier.

Thirukkural says that if we do this, our wishes can be obtained immediately.

Not Coveting Another's Wealth

In Chapter 3 of his famous book *Psychology of Money: Timeless Lessons on Wealth, Greed and Happiness*, Morgen Housel describes examples of men whose greed, fed by envy, brought disgrace to themselves and their families and cost them their personal freedom (Housel 2020).

In one story that was in the news, a gentleman called Rajat Gupta had one hundred million dollars and wanted to join the billionaire's club.

He committed fraud and started making millions of dollars illegally until he was caught and imprisoned.

Valluvar says:

இறல்ஈனும் எண்ணாது வெ.ஃகின் விறல்ஈனும்
வேண்டாமை என்னுஞ் செருக்கு. (180)

Mindless coveting of another's wealth brings ruin—pride of freedom from greed brings success (180)

"The greed and desire to snatch another's wealth is so mindless that it will bring ruin," says Valluvar. The message in Maxim 180, which refers to Maxim 35, is to eliminate the mental obstacles that hinder the practice of righteousness laid out in *Thirukkural.* Valluvar strikes at the root here; he does not want us to even think of performing any action motivated by greed. He calls out the mindless greed that will bring ruin in its wake. Here, the warning addresses the effects of such a thought when it is translated to action. The consequences are shame and the confiscation of ill-gotten wealth by the law, followed by loss of happiness, reputation, and freedom.

On the contrary, not desiring what is not ours is the basis for instilling self-pride. It is the foundation of success.

We have covered the idea of aRam (the virtuous Path) and the obstacles Valluvar wants us to clear from our minds before we prepare ourselves for its practice. We have seen the obstacles that need to be cleared from our minds to equip us for the journey in the path of aRam. We cannot progress along our path without solving the problems that hinder us. We have seen in this chapter that jealousy, wrath, covetousness, and hateful speech can be controlled and conquered. Next, we will look at the fears, anxieties, and worries that may affect us during our journey to sublimity. We will also see how we can get relief from anxiety.

Summary: Remove envy, greed, and anger. Speak kind words.

3.

**Smiling away Distress
A Body–Mind Approach**

I love those who smile in trouble

– Leonardo da Vinci

F ear and anxiety are typical emotions that we experience in our lives, and how we respond to them depends on our life experiences, awareness, perspective, and our ability to reflect and reframe our beliefs. These emotions warn us of dangerous environments, situations, and relationships. They help keep us safe. These emotions can also affect us when we embark on something untested, significant, life-changing, and impactful. Emotions such as excitement and nervousness can lead to that fluttering sensation known as butterflies in the stomach (Knight 2021). These responses are determined by our physiology, and different people react differently to these emotions.

However, when we experience anxiety and fear, it is a signal that something is brewing. Traumatic past experiences can induce anxiety and the fear that something negative may happen. For some people, these emotions may be triggered without any plausible cause. The panic that anxiety can induce could lead to missed opportunities. It can also affect our health. If we once encounter failure, grief follows. The resulting loss of confidence and fear of failing again can make us reluctant to act. We may feel anxious as the situation that produced the initial failure approaches. Fear can make us recoil from doing things that would make a big difference in our lives. We will never reach our full potential if we get overwhelmed by fear. Further, persistent, unrelenting, immobilizing sensations of fear and anxiety are not normal.

When fear and anxiety are reignited with full force, we freeze or retreat. We will do anything to stop the helpless feeling of being stuck. Sometimes—but not all the time—the right answer is to stop or back up. Fear and anxiety can become a recurring theme in our lives if they consistently prevent us from living a full life and experiencing the thrill of healthy challenges and accomplishments.

Valluvar's Approach to Dealing with Distress

Valluvar devotes a chapter to addressing the fear, anxieties, and distress we described in the previous section. His chapter titled "இடுக்கண் அழியாமை (idukkaN azhiyaamai)" can be translated as "overcoming distress, adversity, and fear of failure." Adversity encompasses mental, physical, and financial challenges such as learning disabilities, memory issues, illness, injuries, difficulty in making friends, dealing with bullies, loss of employment, and career-related difficulties.

Distress tolerance is a psychological skill that requires an individual to withstand, endure, or accept intense emotional suffering, discomfort, or challenging situations without resorting to impulsive or self-destructive behaviors. It focuses on developing strategies and techniques for effectively managing overwhelming emotions and distressing circumstances, the ultimate goal being to prevent impulsive reactions and promote resilience. Distress tolerance skills empower individuals to acknowledge and cope with unpleasant feelings in a healthy and constructive manner, fostering emotional well-being and preventing harmful responses to difficult life situations. A half-smile can help us tolerate distress by improving our ability to accept difficult situations and effectively cope with them (Cognitive Behavioral Therapy Los Angeles 2023).

In his first maxim of Chapter 63, Valluvar wants us to face adversity with a gentle smile. The poet says that the smile is the most powerful tool to combat adversity and emphasizes this point strongly with carefully chosen words. The smile can be put to use immediately and is available at no cost. How does the smile counteract distress? The mechanism is based on the bidirectional nature of behavior and emotions: Most of the time, when we experience a positive emotion, such as joy, we smile because of the joy. However, current cognitive behavioral research has shown that it works the other way, too: Smile for a few minutes, and you will feel happy. Make an angry expression by wrinkling your forehead, and you will feel irritated. Take short, shallow breaths, and you will feel anxious. That is, engage in the behavior, and the corresponding emotion will follow (Gillihan 2018).

இடுக்கண் வருங்கால் நகுக அதனை
அடுத்தூர்வது அஃதொப்பது இல். (621)

**Learn to smile at adversity, what follows
cannot be harder (621)**

Thus, in the first maxim of Chapter 63 (Maxim 621), Valluvar introduces a powerful technique to combat adversity and overcome distress. In this maxim, Valluvar suggests that a mindful smile can help alleviate the negative effects of adversity. He says the experience of facing challenges is like a game that we must play. He encourages us to face sorrow and defeat with a determined and rational mindset. Maxim 622, Valluvar's first training lesson, is aimed at strengthening our distress tolerance. He wants us to cultivate the wisdom and skills necessary to handle sorrows and debacles. By slowly building our strength and resolve to overcome adversity, he encourages us to pick a battle, tease anxiety, and stare fear down. He wants us to persevere to reach our destiny and achieve our goals slowly but surely like a bullock cart traversing rough terrain (Maxim 624). The smile technique helps us overcome setbacks and remain determined even when facing multiple challenges.

In the chapter that addresses strengthening distress tolerance, Valluvar also builds a philosophical foundation that can help alleviate some of our troubles. If we do not value wealth too much, we will not fear financial hardship. Excessive attachment to material things weakens us, and it is only when we start loosening our bonds to these material possessions that we will begin to obtain relief from anxiety. Simply put, losses do not bother the wise, who understand the temporary nature of material comforts (Maxim 626). Valluvar states that moderating our joy when we succeed is another way of developing resilience to failures (628). Lastly, even enemies will admire and respect those who remain resolute in the face of adversity. The wise are mature enough to remain happy even in adversity, and even their enemies admire their spirit (Maxim 630).

Valluvar on Overcoming Difficulties

வெள்ளத் தனைய இடும்பை அறிவுடையான்
உள்ளத்தின் உள்ளக் கெடும் (622)

Sorrows come rolling in like floods, but the wise mind
has ways to overcome them (622)

மடுத்தவா யெல்லாம் பகடன்னான் உற்ற
இடுக்கண் இடர்ப்பாடு உடைத்து (624)

Troubles will vanish before the man who struggles
against difficulties,
just as a bull draws a cart through the deep mire (624)

அற்றேமென்று அல்லற் படுபவோ பெற்றேமென்று
ஓம்புதல் தேற்றா தவர் (626)

People who do not cherish wealth are
unlikely to be concerned when they lose (626)

இன்பம் விழையான் இடும்பை இயல்பென்பான்
துன்பம் உறுதல் இலன் (628)

People who do not crave pleasure and understand that
adversity is a natural part of life are not affected by
adversity (628)

இன்னாமை இன்பம் எனக்கொளின்
ஆகுந்தன்
ஒன்னார் விழையுஞ் சிறப்பு (630)

Adversaries respect those who can remain happy even in adversity (630)

The Half-Smile: A Cognitive Behavior Therapy Technique

Cognitive behavior is understood as the interconnection between our emotions, thoughts, actions, and body sensations. Our thoughts can affect our feelings and actions. For example, we may avoid a situation due to the fear of being judged boring. In a therapeutic treatment approach called Cognitive Behavior Therapy (CBT), problem-solving skills are used to cope with difficult situations.

The strategy used is to face fears and adversities rather than avoiding them. Patients are taught to calm their minds and relax.

The goal is for the individual to assume the role of their own therapist. This therapy focuses on finding ways to help individuals cope with current stressors rather than on finding out what led to their difficulties.

The half-smile as a stress reduction technique is now part of today's wellness practice in CBT (Kraft and Pressman 2012).

The training protocols were established by psychologists after many experimental outcomes demonstrated positive effects. In one such experiment, chopsticks were used to activate the facial muscles and simulate smiles. The experimental group was tasked with the voluntary smile protocol.

Facial muscles were activated using this technique, and the heart rate was monitored. After performing a stressful task, the heart rates of smiling people reverted to resting levels faster than those of their non-smiling counterparts.

Smiling helped the subjects quickly reduce their heart rate from panic levels.

Thirukkural has given us a couple of effective methods of strengthening our distress tolerance in the form of mystical insights.

In the next chapter, we will explore Valluvar's mystical insights into the connection between eye movement and the mind.

Summary: The smile heals and builds distress tolerance.

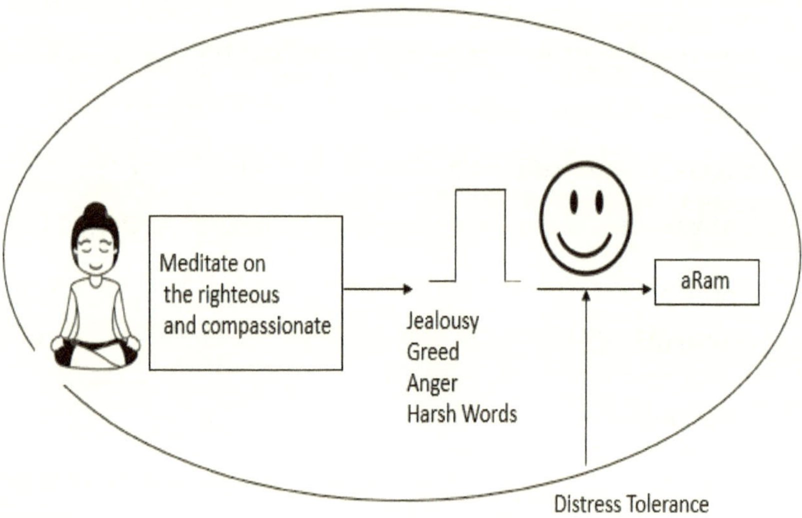

4.

Eye Movement and The Mind A Mystical Insight

arlier in this book, we read about Valluvar's *Supreme Being.* Valluvar wants us to meditate by focusing on the virtuous and compassionate Supreme Being. The entire masterpiece is held together by the themes of virtue and compassion. We can now begin to see how Valluvar's Supreme Being manifests in the world. Valluvar does not preach that the Supreme Being watches from the heavens to check if His subjects follow a code book or moral diktats. Valluvar's Supreme Being does not perform incredible miracles such as bringing a dead man back to life. His Supreme Being manifests in the world through the practice of virtue and compassion. One of Valluvar's maxims even places a human being who practices love and virtue on the same plane as celestials. Valluvar's Supreme Being is both accessible and understandable. All the enigmas play out on Mother Earth (*vaiyam*) itself, and mysteries are unraveled as we proceed through his chapters.

Recently, I read an instructive story about the compassion shown by children to their class teacher. The teacher, Ms. X, was diagnosed with cancer and had taken a lot of time off from school. She had lost her nice wavy hair due to the treatment. While she was recovering from her treatment, one of her colleagues visited Ms. X, who told her she was uncomfortable about returning to school with her new bald look. However, she was seeking a purpose in life and was eager to leave her home and continue to work on a part-time basis. Her bald appearance was holding her back. Her teacher friend discussed this with the children in her class. After a discussion, all the children agreed to shave their heads and welcome their teacher back to school. The kids were overjoyed when they saw their teacher, and the class had an enjoyable time. For Ms. X, the day she returned to school turned out be a joyous day. All her worries about her bald appearance disappeared when she saw the love and compassion exhibited by the children of her class. The empathy and comradery of her students had succeeded in normalizing a condition she had been sad about, and this transformation brought her great joy. She went back home with a twinkle in her eyes, looking forward to working again.

Valluvar uses the word *kaNNOttam* to denote "exhibiting empathy." Valluvar makes this quality an important attribute of his model citizen, called Sanron. The word literally means "movement of the eyes." kaNNOttam is based on the idea of expressing love and compassion through observation with our eyes as we work toward reducing suffering and forgiving others' faults. We see how nations rush to help each other during disasters such as tsunamis and earthquakes. The same human quality impels people to rush to the rescue when they witness accidents on roads. This quality and character are essential at both the individual and social levels.

If we have this quality, we will be able to live without hurting others; moreover, we will be able to forgive others' faults. We will also be able to help people in distress. Not just ordinary men and women but also those in leadership positions can demonstrate this quality. When trying to behave in a mindfully compassionate way, we could fall short of our ideals; we may also face problems. Regardless, the emphasis should be on accepting, persevering, forgiving, and moving on.

Modern Science on Eye Movements

As humans, we rely predominantly on our sense of sight to understand the world around us. The images we see with our eyes are entirely dependent on how our brain processes them. The eyes are thought to play an important role in the ability to accurately infer others' feelings (empathic accuracy), which is an important skill for social interaction.

Although full face vision allows for more accurate identification of emotions, eye-tracking studies have shown that the eyes are most often observed during emotion processing, suggesting a crucial role for the eyes in transmitting important cues.

The eyes express all the emotions and states of the mind and body. They soften in love, harden with anger, widen in fear, narrow in suspicion, roll in exasperation, glaze with boredom, and weep in sadness. The eyes hold a special importance among the body's organs. "Eyes are bold as lions—roving, running, leaping, here and there, far and near," wrote the American philosopher Ralph Waldo Emerson in his 1860 collection of essays, *The Conduct of Life* (emersoncentral.com n.d.). The concept of eyes being windows into the mind is supported by research in medicine: changes in eyes or vision can provide clues about neurological or psychiatric disorders, says Marcus Woo in his article in *Nature* (Woo 2019).

In an exciting new research direction, Liao et al. are using eye movement recordings to discover treatment options for persons with **Parkinson's disease**, a brain disorder that leads to bodily tremors and other movement deficits (Byers Eye Institute 2021). Persons with Parkinson's disease tend to have abnormal eye movement patterns. Liao et al. have measured eye movement behavior in hundreds of subjects with a variety of vision and eye movement issues. Their research is one of the first to investigate how eye and brain diseases affect visual functions such as reading or watching scenery on a digital screen (Byers Eye Institute 2021).

Compassion and Forbearance

We may visit an optometrist to check our vision and find that we have perfect 20/20 vision, but we may still be unable to understand visual cues that more empathic people easily understand. We may have other shortcomings. Recent studies have found that the eyes can yield insights into neurological issues. Recent studies on individuals with Alzheimer's disease have confirmed changes in eye movements associated with pathology. Researchers have also detected differences in eye movements associated with empathetic responses.

Another team at Stanford University is using eye movement recordings to discover treatment options for persons with Parkinson's disease. Persons with this disease tend to exhibit abnormal eye movement patterns. Researchers have measured eye movement behavior in hundreds of subjects with a variety of vision and eye movement issues.

Valluvar calls unfeeling eyes sore spots.

கண்ணிற்கு அணிகலம் கண்ணோட்டம் அஃதின்றேல்

புண்ணென்று உணரப் படும் (575)

Kind looks add beauty to the eyes; without reflected feelings,

they are just sore spots of pain (575)

In Valluvar's time, we could not study the structure of the nerves and the brain; today, we have the necessary technology. Infrared cameras and computer programs have also simplified eye tracking. In the last few years, research has shown that eye tracking can reveal the stage of an individual's thought process. We can study how the inability to process feelings based on sight affects eye movements. Valluvar simply called this inability to bestow kindness with the eyes a sore (கண்ணோட்டம் இல்லாமை).

Compassion and Forbearance Hold the World in Its Place

A well-known Tamil poet of the 19th century, Subramanya Bharathi, wrote:

My heart bleeds when your eyes weep,

Oh, light of my life,

my life is yours; I live for you

The eyes convey so much kindness, love, and empathy. The above lines explain how the eyes are an index of the mind.

The Tamil word kaNNOttam (kaN-eye), which literally means "run of the eye" or "movement of the eye," depicts a mind full of kindliness.

Persons with kaNNOttam have graceful minds that express sympathy through their eyes. They understand the plight of the suffering and have a kind disposition toward others. Valluvar says:

கண்ணோட்டம் என்னும் கழிபெருங் காரிகை
உண்மையான் உண்டிவ் வுலகு. (571)

The world sustains itself without complete destruction as
it has a beauty called compassion (571)

The world exists as it is because some of us, especially our leaders, possess kaNNOttam. Otherwise, our world would be an "an eye for an eye" kind of jungle. People with kaNNOttam can accept apologies, forgive, let go, and move on.

This world is stable because of the beautiful quality called compassion. kaNNOttam (i.e., compassion) encompasses several values that are essential to human relationships, such as forgiveness, compassion, generosity, kindness, love, flexibility, and respect. It is a way of life that encourages individuals to be friendly and give up their own interests in favor of the greater good.

Compassion beautifies the world; indeed, the world exists because of it. kaNNOttam is compassion based on what is seen. Maxim 571 says that the compassionate gaze is a blessing, and that the world's continued survival is thanks to the presence in it of such compassion.

Life cannot thrive without compassion because we are interdependent. The world consists of many kinds of people, some of whom are criminals. If all crime were severely punished, then the world would be a very destructive place. It is kaNNOttam that lubricates the wheels of human relations. kaNNOttam is a cultural asset that enables life to flourish.

Unfeeling Eyes: Lack of Compassion

பண்என்னாம் பாடற்கு இயைபின்றேல்
கண்என்னாம்
கண்ணோட்டம் இல்லாத கண் (573)

Tunes not in accord with the theme of the song and

cold glances are of no avail (573)

Most of us avoid gatherings with loud music and drumming at night, though inebriated people whose senses are dulled may like it. Some of us can end up with a headache. In general, the music must fit the occasion. Otherwise, it is better not to play it.

Valluvar values the ability to empathize with people in distress. When he addresses the subject of kaNNOttam, he expands the scope of his canvas, portraying a graceful nature that expresses empathy with kindly eyes, understands the plight of the suffering, and is kindly disposed toward others.

He describes those without this graceful nature as having unfeeling eyes that show they are life's misfits, just like the tune that does not fit the lyrics and theme of the song.

Summary: The eyes mirror the mind. The word kaNNOttam in Thirukkural conveys compassion and forbearance. Lack of compassion may indicate pathology of the eye and mind.

5.

Gratitude and Forbearance

If you want to find happiness, find gratitude

– Steve Maraboli

Valluvar mentions the mind (*Manam*) and its wellness (*nalam*) in a few places. We have discussed his Godhead and Meditation models earlier. In Chapter 1, we saw how worries are dispelled through meditation. Valluvar presents the idea of aRam as a path in life that we follow by purifying our mind; overcoming jealousy, anger, and greed; and not using harsh words. In the following chapters, we will explore some of the aspects of wellness that he advocates, such as ways to shape our thoughts and behavior. In this chapter, we will look at gratitude and forbearance.

Gratitude

Valluvar defines gratitude as remembering the good deeds of others who have helped us. He places high value on timely help that is given voluntarily, that is, on help that is given even in the absence of an obligation to do so. Failing to render help is considered a deviation from the path of aRam, the righteous way of life. Ingratitude, i.e., failure to acknowledge the timely help rendered by others, is unacceptable.

The world operates smoothly thanks to mutual assistance. Our own efforts are complemented by the help we receive, which enriches our life. Unexpected setbacks can occur at any time, and we may find it difficult to overcome adversity alone. Hence, we are obligated by aRam to express our gratitude for the help we have received from others.

நன்றி மறப்பது நன்றன்று நன்றல்லது
அன்றே மறப்பது நன்று (108)

**Do not forget help received—but to forget
the "not so good" is healthy (108)**

Research has shown that consciously practicing gratitude can reduce stress and anxiety. In fact, studies have found that a single act of thoughtful gratitude immediately increases happiness and reduces depression. These effects disappeared within three to six months, so we should practice gratitude repeatedly (Emmons 2008).

According to the mental health curriculum, a protective factor is defined as something that decreases the chances of a person being negatively affected by a situation or condition (National Research Council (US) and Institute of

Medicine (US) Committee on the Prevention of Mental Disorders and Substance Abuse Among Children, Youth, and Young Adults: Research Advances and Promising Interventions 2009).

The practice of gratitude is considered an effective protective factor that can help in many situations, including mental health challenges like depression and anxiety, or substance use challenges.

For Valluvar, gratitude is about counting even the smallest blessing conferred on us or help received by us. *Thinai* (fox millet) is a small millet with a tiny grain, a short-term crop.

According to Valluvar, if we understand the value of gratitude, we would cherish and value even the smallest help rendered to us (help that is as small as a millet (*Thinai*)) as though it were as large as the *Panai* (the tall palm).

The palm grows tall and lives long. Similarly, let us be grateful for any help rendered to us, however small it may be, and may it live long in our memory.

திணைத்துணை நன்றி செயினும்
பனைத்துணையாக்
கொள்வர் பயன்தெரி வார் (104)

Though help conferred may be as small as a
millet grain,
To the discerning its benefits will be as large as
the palmyra (104)

Instead of being consumed by all that is going wrong in our lives, we can begin to practice gratitude by thinking of all that we need to be thankful for, such as family and friends, our home, or a beautiful sunny day. Writing these thoughts down or saying them aloud can help us stay positive during difficult times.

At the neurobiological level, gratitude regulates the sympathetic nervous system, which activates our anxiety responses. At the psychological level, gratitude conditions the brain to filter out negative thoughts and focus on positive thoughts (Chowdhury 2019).

Another important aspect of practicing gratitude is celebrating small wins. We often become preoccupied with celebrating major milestones such as a new job, marriage, or purchasing a house. Although these major achievements should be celebrated, it is equally important to celebrate small wins. Sometimes, simply getting out of bed on a bad day can be cause for celebration!

However, more often than not, our daily lives are full of distractions and stress, and we tend to overlook our small wins. Think about the past few days: what did we achieve that went unacknowledged? Did we cook a delicious meal, start a new book, or chat with a loved one? Take a moment now to celebrate it and express gratitude. In fact, why not write it down in a journal (Byrne 2012)?

Grudges and Forbearance

When we feel wronged, we tend to hold on to the feeling as a grudge. We could still be angry about an unfortunate incident, but the person concerned may have forgotten about it. We recall the incident whenever we meet that person. Holding on to negative feelings for too long can become habitual, which is not healthy whether we express our displeasure or keep it to ourselves.

Holding a grudge—whatever our intentions or the cause of our bitterness—can hurt us, regardless of our intentions or the reason for our bitterness. Clinging to anger can impact us emotionally, physically, and socially, so it is important to learn to let go of our grudges and cope with anger in a healthier way.

Holding on to grudges can harm our mental health in a variety of ways. Most importantly, harboring anger will, in general, only make us more angry. Holding on to negative experiences instead of moving on or finding an acceptable resolution can trap us in a loop of resentment, bitterness, hopelessness, emptiness, and rage.

In the earlier verse (108) on gratitude, Valluvar recommends not to forget help received, but to forget "not so good" events. Maxim 152 states that tolerating negative events is good, but forgetting them is even better (அதனினும் நன்று). Simply put, harboring negative feelings exposes us to unpleasant emotions and thoughts, which can skew our mindset toward negativity, either slowly or abruptly. Focusing on negativity can harm our well-being.

பொறுத்தல் இறப்பினை என்றும் அதனை
மறத்தல் அதனினும் நன்று (152)

**Bear with hurt caused by transgressions—better
to forget it completely (152)**

Repeatedly reliving negative incidents and emotions can
be upsetting, exhausting, and frustrating, because nothing
gets resolved or changes, except, perhaps, that we end up
feeling more enraged or hurt. In fact, studies show that
brooding on an unpleasant event makes it feel as though
the incident happened much more recently than it actually
did (Vanbuskirk 2023).

Studies show that holding on to anger instead of
responding with forgiveness or moving on can have
profound negative effects on physical health as well, likely
due to the added stress that harboring grudges creates.
According to Angela Buttimer, a licensed psychotherapist
(Piedmont Healthcare n.d.): "Living in a chronic state of
tension disables your body's repair mechanisms, increasing
inflammation and the stress hormone cortisol in the body.
Forgiveness engages the parasympathetic nervous system,
which helps our immune system function more efficiently

and makes room for feel-good hormones like serotonin and oxytocin."

Studies have confirmed the benefits of Valluvar's advice not to take revenge. Studies confirm that the actual execution of revenge exacts a bitter cost in terms of time, emotional and physical energy, and even lives. That minute before the revenge is sweet, as the authors of the study recognized. But what about the days and weeks that follow?

ஒறுத்தார்க்கு ஒருநாளை இன்பம்
பொறுத்தார்க்குப்
பொன்றுந் துணையும் புகழ் (156)

Retaliation can yield temporary joy—but forbearance gives lasting glory (156)

In recent years, psychologists have identified several ways in which retribution fails to meet the expectations of the avenger. Behavioral scientists have found that retribution, rather than quenching hostility, can make things worse by prolonging the unpleasantness of the original wrong. They have also found that merely injuring the offender is not sufficient to appease a person's vengeful soul and that retribution frequently feeds a cycle of reprisals.

In his study on the consequences of revenge (Carlsmith et al. 2008), Carlsmith says: "People erroneously believe revenge will make them feel better and help them gain closure. Punishers ruminate on their deed and feel worse than those who cannot avenge a wrong. I think uncertainty prolongs and enhances emotional experiences, and one of the things that avengers do unintentionally is to prolong the unpleasant encounter. Those who don't have a chance to take revenge are forced, in a sense, to move on and focus on something different. And they feel happier."

The benefits of gratitude, forgiveness, and forgetting the wrongs committed against us are numerous.

Thirukkural's guidelines on gratitude and forgetting grudges correlate with mindful practices recommended by psychologists.

Summary: Gratitude is a mindfulness practice. Practicing gratitude and forgetting wrongs can lead to happiness.

6.

Cultivating Our Mind for Success

In order to shape your life, the way you want, and make the changes you desire, you must start making changes in your mind. You need to change your thoughts. Shaping your external life starts from within, in your mind.

– Remez Sassoon

In order to shape your life, the way you want, and make the changes you desire, you must start making changes in your mind. You need to change your thoughts. Shaping your external life starts from within, in your mind. – Remez Sassoon

Valluvar had a great idea about the power of thoughts to shape our minds and actions. He repeatedly appeals to his readers to think (எண்ணுக, உள்ளுக). Earlier, we discussed his Godhead and Meditation models, which feature in many of his maxims. By acquiring learning skills, meditating to free ourselves of worries, avoiding falsehood, not becoming greedy and envious, and being grateful and forgiving, we prepare and condition our minds for success in worldly and business activities. We will discuss couplets in which Valluvar takes us through the steps to achieve success in our ventures.

Strength of Mind

Valluvar believes that "strength of the mind is the ability to act on a plan and complete the associated tasks (661)." Only those with great strength of mind can devise a plan and carry out the associated tasks. Firm commitment and steely resolve are needed to overcome setbacks and disappointments and carry out the tasks.

வினைத்திட்பம் என்பது ஒருவன் மனத்திட்பம்
மற்றைய எல்லாம் பிற (661)

Strength of the mind has the power to succeed,
in its absence
all other capacities falter and fail (661)

To cultivate this mental strength (*manaththitpam*), he recommends that we practice living up to our words. It is easy to make claims about difficult tasks and say, "I can do it." Many people commit to completing a task and do not succeed. This may not prevent them from lecturing us about important projects they have been charged with and their determination to complete them. If, however, they are unable to complete the projects, they may lose the respect of their peers. Valluvar must have been a shrewd observer of people. He says it is rare to find someone who can walk the talk and reach the destination. Anyone can indulge in empty talk. One of the ways to build confidence is to define a doable task, estimate the time and resources needed to complete it, plan the subtasks, and persevere to complete them.

Walk the Talk

> சொல்லுதல் யார்க்கும் எளிய அரியவாம்
> சொல்லிய வண்ணம் செயல் (664)

To say how best to do a job is easy;
to follow up and complete it is difficult (664)

Actually, following through and actually *doing* what we claim we will do is great training for the mind. Our intention is not to make anybody feel guilty for not being able to complete a task that was verbally agreed upon. No, we only wish to emphasize the importance of reflecting on the detailed task, redefining it, and analyzing the required resources and the time needed to complete the task. Finally, after determining that we can complete the task, without any fanfare, we publicly commit to executing it. Valluvar, the teacher, helps us by providing guidelines to help plan and execute aspects of a task. We describe these guidelines in the following sections.

Think and Act

Valluvar wants us to think about the task beforehand rather than starting to think about it after announcing it or while it is in progress [467]. The first mistake is failing to give sufficient thought to the task at hand.

எண்ணித் துணிக கருமம் துணிந்தபின்
எண்ணுவம் என்பது இழுக்கு (467)

Deliberate first, then undertake a mission; hesitation
after commitment leads to painful disgrace
(467)

When we try to do something, we should analyze what we will gain from it, what might stop us from doing it, and how we can overcome the obstacles that might arise. We should also consider alternative actions that will bring in the same benefits. We should not act without prior thought. If we act without thinking and obstacles arise, we may not be able to solve the following problems: We may have to give up without achieving our goals and without any contingency plans in hand. Even if we complete what we had planned, the effort expended may outweigh the benefits gained.

Define the Task

Valluvar wants us to be clear about the task. Most companies now have teams that define tasks by studying the associated needs. Wise people clarify all the aspects of a task before they begin, minimizing the risk of failure.

தெளிவி லதனைத் தொடங்கார் இளிவென்னும்
ஏதப்பாடு அஞ்சு பவர். (464)

Those who fear reproach will not commence anything which has not been (thoroughly considered)
and made clear to them (464)

By asking questions and deriving detailed requirements, one can further define what is needed to pursue a task. For example, talking to potential customers can help clear up details about the desired form and factor of a product. For example, we will not consider producing seven-foot mattresses when the median height of adults in the country is less than six feet.

Think and Plan for Resources

After studying the resources needed, we plan the time it will take to complete the task with the appropriate tools and budget. We do not look for tools while the activity is in progress. We would include the budget for the tools and devices needed to complete the task in the proposal. After the approvals come through, we acquire the equipment needed to start the activity. Valluvar also wants us to plan for the duration of the task. Some tasks can be done by one person; others may need a team. Valluvar wants us to plan ahead to ensure success in the given time. We may have to add more staff to complete the project in the given time (675).

பொருள்கருவி காலம் வினையிடனொடு ஐந்தும்

இருள்தீர எண்ணிச் செயல் (675)

Undertake a task after a thoughtful consideration of the (following) five:

money, means, time, execution, and place (675)

Be Mindful of the Task and Plan

Forgetfulness leads to distraction, which in turn leads to loss of attentiveness. Well-planned initiatives need to be executed without forgetting any important details. *Thirukkural* also asserts that a mindful person will easily accomplish all the planned tasks.

Valluvar uses a phrase in Tamil: "uLLiyathu uLLap peRin" (உள்ளியது உள்ளப் பெறின்). It is used to describe the process of internalizing a thought or idea and the ability to recall it whenever required. Valluvar uses this phrase in his chapter on being present and not being forgetful (Chapter 54).

> உள்ளியது எய்தல் எளிதுமன் மற்றுந்தான்
> உள்ளியது உள்ளப் பெறின் (540)

> **We can easily achieve whatever we wish**
>
> **if we are mindful of it (540)**

Mindfulness can help develop a clear and calm intellect that can internalize an idea and remember it. Such a person does not clutter the mind with negative emotions like anger, jealousy, and greed; neither does he or she use harsh words. Such a person is free of anxieties and worries.

Valluvar believes that our ability to complete a task or project depends primarily on our "strength of mind." However, he does not leave us hanging with that thought; he provides clear and thoughtful ways of strengthening our mind, thus equipping us to complete any task that we may choose to take up.

Thus far, we have traveled the path of aRam laid out by Valluvar to promote our wellness through the cultivation of our mind. We are close to the finish line of the journey, whose goal is a sublime mind.

Summary: Success is cultivated by shaping our thoughts and being mindful.

7.

A Sublime Mind

Anything which elevates the mind is sublime. Greatness of matter, space, power, virtue or beauty, are all sublime.

– John Ruskin

In our mindfulness journey through *Thirukkural*, we practiced meditation to eliminate suffering; avoided anger, greed, and envy; cultivated gratitude and forgiveness; and traveled on the path of virtue (aRam) by speaking kindly and showing compassion to others. Valluvar also describes a few other qualities needed to achieve a sublime mind.

Valluvar has a grand, elevated vision for a model citizen, whom he calls *Sanron.*

He attributes superior mental qualities and traits to the Sanron. Valluvar discusses the qualities and characteristics a person should possess for him or her to be considered a Sanron. English does not have a word that is the exact equivalent of Sanron.

Translators have used a range of words to describe a Sanron, and I find "exemplar" to be the most suitable equivalent. Let us call Valluvar's Sanron an exemplar. The English word *exemplar,* which has French and Latin roots, denotes a model of virtue. The Sanron's nobility is expressed by his conduct and by his attitude toward society, which are filled with love.

The exemplar is careful to avoid any action that will bring shame, and never fails to serve the people. His compassion is so great that it has a healing effect on the sick, and he always stands for the truth.

Maxim 983 defines the sublimity of the exemplar as follows:

அன்புநாண் ஒப்புரவு கண்ணோட்டம்
வாய்மையொடு
ஐந்துசால்பு ஊன்றிய தூண் (983)

Love, fear of sin, benevolence, compassionate grace, and truthfulness
are the five pillars that uphold exemplary character (983)

The noted American spiritualist, Ellen White, wrote: "Great wisdom is needed in dealing with diseases caused through the mind. A sore, sick heart and a discouraged mind need mild treatment. Sympathy and tact will often prove a greater benefit to the sick than will the most skillful treatment given in a cold, indifferent way." (White 1905)

Love is the elixir for curing pain. We see this at the individual and family levels. The Sanron is portrayed as having the ability to heal society's pain.

Soothing the Pain of Troubled Minds

Growing up in a violent or unloving environment can create people with troubled minds. Often, such people lash out at those around them and hurt them. Valluvar's take on his model citizen, the Sanron, in Maxim 987 needs to be seen in the above context The poet asks, what is the point of a sublime mind if it cannot cure such people?

இன்னா செய்தார்க்கும் இனியவே
செய்யாக்கால்
என்ன பயத்ததோ சால்பு? (987)

Of what use is sublimity—if

it does not cure those who cause pain? (987)

The sublimity Valluvar refers to is exemplified by Gandhiji's life. A police officer once brutally stomped on Gandhiji's chest before imprisoning him. During his imprisonment, Gandhiji made footwear from leather pieces and gifted it to the policeman upon his release. This unexpected gift put the policeman to shame. Moreover, he was surprised that the footwear was made to size, and queried Gandhiji about it. Gandhiji explained that he had used the scar left on his chest by the policeman's boot to size the footwear (Kanignan n.d.).

Mental Well-Being (*Mana Nalam*)

Valluvar gives us a path to mental wellness through aRam. He develops his guidelines through several chapters, culminating in a description of the ideal citizen, referred to as the Sanron. He wants the Sanron to cultivate friendships and positive influences, while avoiding people who lack goodwill in the community. By carefully fostering a positive environment, one can achieve lasting fame.

மனநலம் மன்னுயிர்க்கு ஆக்கம் இனநலம்
எல்லாப் புகழும் தரும் (457)

Wellness of mind aids survival—the company
of the worthy yields fame (457)

மனநலம் நன்குடையர் ஆயினும்
சான்றோர்க்கு
இனநலம் ஏமாப்பு உடைத்து (458)

Although the Sanron possesses a sublime mind,
a positive environment will strengthen it (458)

Exemplars (Valluvar's model citizens) possess sublime minds due to their impeccable character. Sanrons exhibit a range of admirable qualities, such as a caring nature, fear of doing things that will bring shame, goodwill toward society, compassion, and truthfulness. Still, they would like to secure themselves by forming positive relationships.

Several modern stressors can affect individuals, such as the work environment, bullies in schools, poverty, pollution, and noise pollution. Valluvar calls the wellness of the surroundings and everyone in it *ina_nalam*. Valluvar's maxims show that the Sanron has qualities that naturally lead them to strive for the wellness of their environment. Valluvar says that the wellness we desire cannot be achieved in isolation. We must strive to achieve wellness in our surroundings. Only then will men of exemplary character, those possessing sublime minds, feel secure.

Social Awareness

Social responsibility is an *ethical* framework in which an individual is obliged to work and cooperate with other individuals and organizations. This will benefit the community that will inherit the world that the individual will eventually leave behind (Jensen 2006). Valluvar recognized the significance of advancing a society through healthy interactions among its citizens. IIis model citizen is wise enough to show benevolence (ஒப்புரவு அறிதல்) to members of the larger society. The common good is prioritized over self-interest, and duty to the larger society is highly regarded.

The poet likens wealth in the hands of socially responsible wise men to a community well that is full of water. Wise men desire that all living beings should flourish. They care about the welfare of the entire world (உலகவாம்). A community well is likened to the wealth of such wise men.

ஊருணி நீர்நிறைந் தற்றே உலகவாம்
பேரறி வாளன் திரு (215)

The wealth of a person with worldly wisdom is

like a life-giving well

that sustains a village community (215)

Valluvar does not spare people who lack social responsibility. He calls them out in Maxim 214.

ஒத்தது அறிவான் உயிர்வாழ்வான்
மற்றையான்
செத்தாருள் வைக்கப் படும் (214)

Live a fuller life engaged in benevolence;

otherwise, you'll be considered a corpse (214)

A human being is a member of the larger society. "No man is an island," noted a famous 17th century poet, John Donne. His poem explores how human beings are connected to each other, and how important that connection is for the well-being and survival of any individual. The needs of society and the role of an individual in it are discerned by wise people. Such a wise person is compatible with society and is likened to a living community well. The wise, who are not solely preoccupied with their own possessions and work, become aware of their surroundings and the needs of the people around them. Such persons, who live in harmony with society, have characteristics that make life bloom on this planet. Valluvar says that persons lacking this goodwill for others are as good as dead even though they may breathe.

The wise person understands that people need food to satisfy their hunger, education to gain knowledge, a residence for shelter, and medicines to treat illness. The wise understand this; they want those around them to live well by possessing what they, the wise, have (ஒத்தது அறிவான்). The wise also identify with those around them by empathizing with their grief and sorrows.

கைமாறு வேண்டா கடப்பாடு மாரிமாட்டு
என்ஆற்றுங் கொல்லோ உலகு (211)

Sublime people expect no return for their dutiful service.

How can the world ever repay the rain cloud? (211)

Rain pours down on the parched land and helps create life on Earth by providing sustenance to many life-forms. Likewise, an enlightened person (i.e., a Sanron: one who is aware of his duty to society) will respond to situations without expecting any reward.

Blessed with the wisdom to live harmoniously in society and aware of its needs, sublime people expect no reward for their benevolence. The wealth in their hands is like the water filling a community well; it serves the entire community.

The Sublime Mind, Truth, and Nonviolence

Sublime people have an honesty that is in tune with the inner workings of their mind. They believe that speaking the truth should not cause harm (*vaaymai*), and Valluvar judges such language more exalted than penance accompanied by charity. Truth follows nonviolence and aligns with all the qualities of the Sanron.

> மனத்தொடு வாய்மை மொழியின் தவத்தொடு
> தானஞ்செய் வாரின் தலை (295)

> IIe who speaks the truth with his heart is
> more exalted than one who does penance and
> charity (295)

Sanrons have sublime minds that make the world around them calm and happy. *Thirukkural* gives more details on the sublimity of the Sanron, which is upheld by the pillars of love, kindness, compassion, dutiful benevolence, fear of causing harm, and truthfulness. The characteristics of Sanrons do not depend on economic status or education. They do not believe in violence; instead, they disarm their enemies through sheer kindness. Strength of mind is developed over a period, and even the Sanron's mother may come to know of this development only later in life after her child has earned a badge of honor from society.

Summary: The sublimity of a Sanron is the ultimate honor that accompanies wellness of mind. The Sanron is free from greed, anger, envy, and hateful words. The Sanron is also compassionate, grateful, gracious, forgiving, healing, truthful, socially responsible, and harms nobody. The sublime mind of the Sanron serves society without expecting any reward, much like the rain.

8.

Putting It All Together

Following the path of **aRam** (Virtue) leads to happiness. We encounter many distractions and experience much distress during our journey through life. Meditation clears our minds and gives us the mental strength to work on the challenging tasks that await us as we journey along our path. This starting point is not emphasized in many commentaries on *Thirukkural* and its translations. I often found myself confused, not understanding the route or the map Valluvar had prepared for me personally. I have sometimes felt helpless due to the lack of clarity surrounding the many prevailing faith systems. Although these ideas were conceived and developed by great saints, I found them too complex and difficult to understand.

Later, the latter-day mystics I quoted from in the first chapter introduced me to Valluvar's mystic symbolism, which helped me understand the value of devotional meditation.

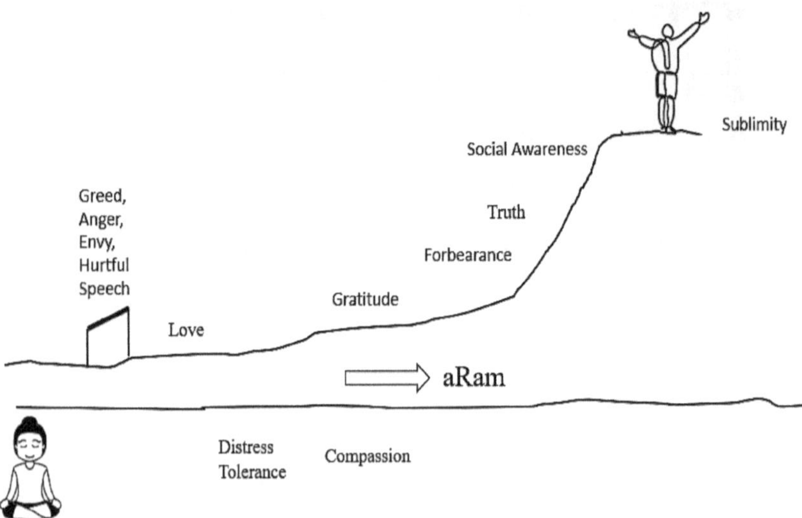

Valluvar's secular tone and language attracted me to *Thirukkural*. However, I still struggled to connect the dots regarding the details of how Valluvar laid the foundation for the development of our mental well-being. While studying this, I also discovered insights into Valluvar's use of the smile to improve tolerance to distress. He has devoted a chapter to addressing how we can work on our ability to combat distress and overcome setbacks.

The last difficult idea I confronted was my inability to easily forget disappointments and grudges. I felt relieved after I learned to accept my personal shortcomings. Valluvar's perspective on greed, anger, and jealousy as a destructive barrier to mindfulness becomes clearer when we approach the path laid out with a clear mind. Finally, Valluvar wants us all to be exemplars, role models in society. This is primarily achieved by developing awareness of our environment and the people around us, and by practicing gratitude, compassion, love, kindness, and social awareness.

May you benefit as much from the ideas described here as I have!

References

References

Bryne, R. 2012. The Secret (3). Atria Books.

Byers Eye Institute. 2021. "An Eye–Brain Connection." In Vision Matters: 2021 Annual Report. https://med.stanford.edu/content/dam/sm/ophthalmology/annual-reports/2021_AnnualReport.pdf.

Calm. n.d. "The Neuroscience of Meditation." Calm Blog. https://blog.calm.com/blog/the-neuroscience-of-meditation.

Carlsmith, K.M., T.D. Wilson, and D.T. Gilbert. 2008. "The Paradoxical Consequences of Revenge." Journal of Personality and Social Psychology 95 (6): 1316. https://doi.org/10.1037/a0012165.

Caz, V. n.d. "Finding Clarity in the Fog of Depression & Anxiety." The Guided Meditation Site. https://www.the-guided-meditation-site.com/finding-clarity-in-the-fog-of-depression-anxiety.html.

Chowdhury, M.R. 2019. "The Neuroscience of Gratitude and Effects on the Brain." PositivePsychology.Com. https://positivepsychology.com/neuroscience-of-gratitude/.

Coelho, S. 2022. "Can't Stop Thinking About Past Mistakes? 3 Tips to Stop Ruminating." PsychCentral. https://psychcentral.com/blog/how-to-stop-ruminating-on-the-past.

Cognitive Behavioral Therapy Los Angeles. 2023. "Reduce Emotional Distress with Half Smile | DBT Half-Smile Skill." Cognitive Behavioral Therapy Los Angeles. https://cogbtherapy.com/cbt-blog/2013/07/turn-that-mood-upside-down-with.html.

Emersoncentral.com. n.d. "Ralph Waldo Emerson 'The Conduct of Life': Complete Text." Ralph Waldo Emerson. https://emersoncentral.com/texts/the-conduct-of-life/.

Emmons, R.A. 2008. Thanks!: How Practicing Gratitude Can Make You Happier. Houghton Mifflin Company.

Jaffe, E. 2011. "The Complicated Psychology of Revenge." APS Observer, October 4. https://www.psychologicalscience.org/observer/the-complicated-psychology-of-revenge.

Gelpi, J. 2023. "A Guide to Mindful Living: The 5 Senses Grounding Technique." Balance. https://balanceapp.com/blog/5-senses-grounding-technique.

Gillihan, S.J. 2020. Cognitive Behavioural Therapy Made Simple: 10 Strategies for Managing Anxiety, Depression, Anger, Panic and Worry. Hachette UK.

Housel, M. 2020. The Psychology of Money: Timeless lessons on wealth, greed, and happiness. Harriman House. Jensen, D. 2006. "What Does It Mean To Be Responsible?" From the chapter titled "Responsibility," p. 675. In Endgame, Volume 2: The Problem of Civilization. Vol. 2. New York: Seven Stories Press. https://derrickjensen.org/endgame/responsible-what-does-it-mean/.

Kanignan. n.d. "குறள்திறன் ". Kuralthiran. https://kuralthiran.com/KuralThiran/KuralThiran0987.aspx

Knight, B. 2021. "Fear and Anxiety In The Human Design Chart And What You Can Do About It." Brigitte Knight Coaching. https://brigitteknight.com/blog/fear-anxiety-gates-of-human-design-chart.

Kuppusamy, R. 2022. Thirukkural: Spiritual Commentary. Society for Immortality Research Limited.

Kraft, T.L., and S.D. Pressman. 2012. "Grin and Bear It: The Influence of Manipulated Facial Expression on the Stress Response." Psychological Science.

Lutz, A., L.L. Greischar, N.B. Rawlings, M. Ricard, and R.J. Davidson. 2004. "Long-Term Meditators Self-Induce High-Amplitude Gamma Synchrony during Mental Practice." Proceedings of the National Academy of Sciences 101 (46). National Academy of Sciences: 16369–73. https://doi.org/10.1073/pnas.0407401101.

Maugham, Somerset. 1958. Points of View. London: Heinemann.

Narayanasamy, J. 2008. Thirukural: Transliteration and Translation. Chennai: Sura Publications.

National Research Council (US) and Institute of Medicine (US) Committee on the Prevention of Mental Disorders and Substance Abuse Among Children, Youth, and Young Adults: Research Advances and Promising Interventions. 2009. Preventing Mental, Emotional, and Behavioural Disorders among Young People: Progress and Possibilities. Edited by M. Ellen, T. O'Connell, and E. Kenneth. Washington, D.C.: National Academies Press (US). https://www.ncbi.nlm.nih.gov/books/NBK32775/.

Piedmont Healthcare. n.d. "What Does Holding a Grudge Do to Your Health?" Piedmont. https://www.piedmont.org/living-real-change/what-does-holding-a-grudge-do-to-your-health. Accessed June 2, 2024.

Ricard, M., A. Lutz, and R. Davidson. 2014. "Neuroscience Reveals the Secrets of Meditation's Benefits." Scientific American 311 (5): 38–45. https://www.scientificamerican.com/article/neuroscience-reveals-the-secrets-of-meditation-s-benefits.

Vanbuskirk, S. 2023. "The Mental Health Effects of Holding a Grudge." Verywell Mind. https://www.verywellmind.com/the-mental-health-effects-of-holding-a-grudge-5176186.

Walsh, R. 1999. Essential Spirituality: The Seven Central Practices. NewYork: Wiley.

Walsh, R., and S.L. Shapiro. 2006. "The Meeting of Meditative Disciplines and Western Psychology: A Mutually Enriching Dialogue." American Psychologist 61 (3). American Psychological Association: 227. https://doi.org/10.1037/0003-066X.61.3.227.

White, E.G. 1905. The Ministry of Healing.
Woo, M. 2019. "Eyes Hint at Hidden Mental-Health Conditions." Nature. https://www.nature.com/articles/d41586-019-01114-9.

About the author

Kathiravan Krishnamurthi, Ph.D., was born in Coimbatore, Tamil Nadu, India. After obtaining his B.E. (Honours) from National Institute of Technology (NIT) Tiruchirappalli (then Regional Engineering College (REC) Trichy), he came to Canada to earn his M.S and Ph.D. in Electronics. He has served both the communications and electronics industries in various capacities over the years. Mainly tasked with the design of new circuits and systems, his various designs have resulted in several commercial products and more than 14 patents.

He pursues his interest in Tamil through translation and transcreation. His Tamil book, *Fundamentals of Radio Communications* (அடிப்படை ரேடியோ தொடர்பாடல்), was nominated for the best technical book of 2013 by the Tamil Nadu Government. He collaborated with a team of enthusiasts to compile another Tamil book, அறிவியல் அறிவோம் (*Let Us Get to Know Science*), which focuses on teaching student's day-to-day science. His third Tamil book, *Science through Stories* (கதைவிழி அறிவியல்), is slated to be published this year. His latest work, *Thirukkural: A Snapshot of the Sastras?* is in English. This book, a refutation of Nagaswamy's polemical book *Thirukural: An Abridgement of Sastras* and a detailed study of Thirukkural and its lessons, is based on a series of articles he wrote in many forums and is informed by his reading and understanding of the classic commentaries.

Kathiravan currently lives in Westford, Massachusetts, United States.